CARLIE MILLER

101 At Home Date Night Ideas

Home-Based Date Ideas for After the Kids Go to Bed

First edition

This book was professionally typeset on Reedsy.
Find out more at reedsy.com

Contents

Introduction

Finding the time and money for a date night out on the town can be tough. Maybe it's difficult to find a babysitter or maybe you're looking to save some money. Just because going out for a date every week might not be feasible doesn't mean that you can't still have a date night! The perfect time to spend some quality time with your partner may be just under your noses - after the kids are in bed. Take advantage of this time!

The benefits of a date night are numerous - it helps to break up your day to day routines, you get to spend time connecting with your partner, and it'll help you to build new memories together. Win-win for everyone.

In this book you'll find 101 ideas for having a memorable date night at home. The ideas range from creative to romantic, fun to eye-opening. All of the ideas you can do at home, and most of them are very budget-friendly! Whether you have kids or not, these ideas are a great way to spark something new in your relationship. Maybe you'll do something new together that you've never done before, or you'll learn something new about each other, or you'll just have a lot of fun. I challenge you to see how many of these ideas you can do. Some may take you out of your comfort zone, but I assure you it'll be worth it.

The Ideas

Food & Cooking

1. Bake cupcakes together. Only, this idea has a twist. One of you is chosen to do all of the mixing and measuring, blindfolded! The person without the blindfold must give verbal instructions and hand the blindfolded person everything they need - the ingredients, utensils, etc. See how they turn out! Or, for a different idea, bake cupcakes together and then decorate them while each wearing a blindfold.

2. Cook a fancy meal together. Find a recipe that sounds tasty, get all of the ingredients and spend some time in the kitchen together. Use nice dishes, light candles and dim the lights. Take turns sharing things you love about each other while you eat. Or, talk about some of the favorite meals you've had together.

3. Have a wine (or beer or hard seltzer) tasting. Buy a few bottles and try a little of each. Or, buy an at-home tasting kit from a company like Voluptuary Wines. They'll ship sample bottles to you for you to try in the comfort of your home. What do you like best? Do you and your partner agree on a favorite? If you want to get fancy, see if you can name any notes you taste.

4. Dine in the dark. Here's a unique experience you probably haven't done before. Order takeout. Turn off the lights. Put on blindfolds. Dig in!

5. Flavor trip using miracle berries. You can buy miracle berry tablets online from websites like Amazon. Consume one tablet each (don't worry, they're completely safe and legal but definitely research if you want to know more), then try eating different foods. Try lemons, goat cheese and bitter chocolate - everything becomes sweeter! Your taste will go back to normal in fifteen minutes to two hours.

6. Have a baking competition with no recipe. Choose a simple baked good, like chocolate chip or sugar cookies. Set out all of the ingredients. Spend your date competing to make the best version of the chosen baked good, but neither of you can follow a recipe. Once your treats are done baking, taste test and decide on a winner.

7. Make your own ice cream using two metal cans. Search online for "ice cream in a can" for the recipe and instructions. Try out your favorite flavors and mix-ins.

8. Have a picnic in your living room. Lay a picnic blanket on your living room or bedroom floor, make a simple (or elaborate) charcuterie board using cheeses, nuts, sausages and fruits, and spend this date pretending to avoid ants in the park. Split a bottle of wine and you'll almost feel it's a warm, sunny summer day.

9. Make fondue together. Choose cheese or chocolate (or both!) and get all of the fixin's. Yum yum!

10. Have a blindfolded taste test. Each person finds five foods from around the home. Make sure to hide these from your partner. Take turns being blindfolded. Whoever is blindfolded has to eat the foods their partner gathered and guess what they are. Who can guess the most? What foods were you surprised you didn't get?

11. Try foods neither of you have eaten. Before the date, head to the grocery store (an international supermarket is a great option). Pick out a few foods neither of you have eaten before. On your date, try all the foods together and see what you think. You may discover a new favorite food!

12. Eat dinner or dessert with your wrists tied together. This will work best if you're sitting across from each other on the floor with your plates of food between the two of you. Use handkerchiefs or soft scarves to tie your wrists together and *bon appetit*!

13. Film your own cooking show. Choose a recipe, prep the ingredients and set up your cameras (phones will do fine). Set one phone across from your workspace on a tripod (or against something steady). The other phone/camera can be used to get close up or overhead shots. Film yourselves cooking and eating a dish you made.. Lean into your new role as a celebrity chef. Come up with catchphrases and be as exuberant or animated as you wish!

14. Do a five-food challenge. Each of you chooses five ingredients from your kitchen. Your partner has to come up with a new recipe using ALL of the ingredients you picked. This one could get tricky if you're trying to combine tuna with bananas and ice cream... so, to make things easier to swallow, you could agree that all ingredients must be either savory or sweet. Once you're both finished, taste test. Whoever's creation tastes the best gets a prize of your choosing (foot massage? A coupon for a homemade meal? Your choice!).

15. Make fancy s'mores together. Roast marshmallows using an outdoor fire pit or on a gas stove. Or, toast the marshmallows in your oven. Try out different gourmet s'mores options like chocolate covered strawberry using Nutella and strawberries, caramel apple with caramel sauce and granny smith apples, or peanut butter cup and banana.

Fun & Games

16. Make up new rules to a game you own. Take a game that you already own and change the rules. For example, new rules for Connect 4 may be that the first player to have two discs of the same color touching loses. The sky's the limit with this one.

17. Play games from the TV show *Minute to Win It*. If you search online for "*Minute to Win It*" games, you'll find a lot of great, 60 second games to play. Each game requires you to do a seemingly simple task (although some are harder than they look!) within 60 seconds. Most of the games require things you likely have around the house. Some favorite games include keeping three balloons in the air for a minute and using chopsticks to stack six iron nuts on top of each other.

18. Build a blanket fort. This one is a classic but maybe it's been awhile since you've done this. Gather up all of the blankets and pillows in your home and make a cozy spot for the two of you. Put on your pajamas and snuggle up while watching a favorite movie or TV show.

19. Play a collaborative video game together. Use any console you have or even just your phones. Some well-rated options are Snipper Clips, Operation: Tango, Overcooked and It Takes Two.

20. Make your own truth or dare Jenga. Buy a Jenga game and write out truth or dare questions on each block with permanent market. Once you've written questions on each block, play the game with your partner and see what happens.

21. Play the game *Keep Talking and Nobody Explodes*. Oh no! A bomb's about to go off, and you'll need to work with your partner to diffuse the bomb. The catch? Only one person can see the bomb, and the other player has to relay instructions for diffusing it by reading a bomb defusal manual. You'll really have to work as a team to... well, not explode. The game is available for VR, Android, iPhone, Switch, and other platforms as well.

22. Play hide and go seek. To make it more challenging, set a timer for two minutes. The hider and the seeker both only get 120 seconds to hide and to seek. Play a few rounds, reducing the amount of time you each get - from two minutes to one minute to thirty seconds.

23. Make your own mini golf course. Use different items around your home like yoga mats, mugs, curtain rods, etc. to set up a few different holes. Play using an actual golf putter and golf ball or get creative and use what you have around the home.

24. Make paper airplanes. Fold some sheets of printer paper until you've created a few airplanes. Spend your date competing to see whose plane flies the farthest, or highest, or hits the walls the least. There are many ways to make a paper airplane. Decide on the design on your own or look up designs at foldnfly.com.

25. Put together a Lego kit. Borrow one from your kids or buy one just for your date night. It can be elaborate or simple - the fun here is spending quality time with your partner while collaborating and building something together.

26. Have an adult kids birthday party. Play pin the tail on the donkey, bat at a piñata, exchange gifts with each other, and eat a cartoon-themed sheet cake.

27. Play Jackbox games. If you haven't heard of Jackbox games, you're in for a treat. Best known as a digital party game, this game can also be played with just two people. The best two player Jackbox games are Trivia Murder Party, Bomb Corp, Fibbage, Guesspionage, and Zeeple Dome.

28. Play virtual reality games. Have a VR headset already? Great! If not, you can buy a cheap adapter online to turn your phone into a VR headset. With the adapter, you can watch 360 videos on YouTube (try out a roller coaster video). With a standalone headset, you can play games together and get to know your partner's avatar while bowling, swimming in Half and Half, or playing Pierhead Arcade.

29. Try out movieoke. Watch a movie or TV show on mute. Turn on subtitles and read them as though you're the character speaking. This one works the best if there's just one or two characters speaking. A fun alternative to karaoke.

30. Learn card tricks together. Spend some time (before the date or during) learning a card trick. Transform your date into a magic show and share the trick you learned with your partner and be amazed! Remember, magicians never reveal their secrets.

31. Have a murder mystery party, just the two of you. While you may think of murder mysteries as a group or party activity, there are many two-person kits available. If you search online for "murder mystery date night" you'll find several options for your at-home date night. Dress in character, set the scene and have fun sleuthing together.

Looking to the Future

32. Make a couples' bucket list. Include all of the places you want to go, things you want to see and do, and everything you want to accomplish together. This can be an ever-evolving list. Continually check off the things you've done and add more if you come up with new ideas.

33. Search for your dream home together. Talk about what you'd like in a home if you could have everything you'd want. Look for plots of land you could build on, and use websites like Zillow to gander at homes for sale.

34. Spend time creating relationship goals. These could be short-term (for the next week or month) or long-term (for the next several years). Some examples: Go on a dream vacation to Europe, organize the garage, commit to one date night a week over the next two months. It could be anything!

35. Plan to redecorate a room in your home. Create an inspiration board with clippings from magazines, or create a digital board using Pinterest and pin ideas you like. Choose a color palette and a few furniture pieces, as well as wall art, rugs, decorations, and anything else that would give the room a refresh.

Memories & Connection

36. Write down memories you have together. Take turns reading them out loud and reminisce. Save these to read again later and keep adding to them over the weeks, months, and years. Feeling stuck for ideas? Pull up photos on your phone of the two of you to jog your memory.

37. Make a couples time capsule. Include photos of the two of you, tickets to events you've been to, and notes or cards you've given each other. Or, make a digital time capsule by putting files onto a thumb drive. Include pictures, videos, emails and messages you want to remember. Put the time capsule at the back of your closet and include a note with when it should be opened. One year from now? Ten years? Thirty years? You choose!

38. Take turns answering a card deck of questions for couples. Search online for "question card deck for couples," and you'll find a lot of options. The Intimacy Deck by BestSelf Co is a great choice. Their Date Deck and Relationship Deck are also popular. For something different, buy a blank deck of cards from Amazon and use them to write your own set of questions for a future date night.

39. Record the story of how you met. Using the voice recorder on your phone, collaboratively tell the details of how the two of you met. Or, go in separate rooms and each record the story separately. Then, listen to the stories together and see how they're alike and how they differ.

40. Start a shared journal. Keep it on your nightstand or someplace where your kids won't find it. Take turns writing messages to each other for your partner to find.

41. Write letters to your future selves. Either write letters to each other on paper and then seal the envelope, or you can use the website futureme.org. Futureme lets you write an email to yourself that the company will send to you at a date you choose in the future. One month from now? Ten years from now? Take your pick. You can have the letter sent to yourself or to your partner.

42. Recreate your first date at home. This one could be easier or harder depending on your first date. Was it dinner at an Italian restaurant? Make pasta and drink wine at home. Was it coffee and a walk around a park? Brew coffee with a french press and hold hands while taking a slow walk around your yard. You may need to be creative with this one to make it work, but it'll be a fun way to remember your beginnings as a couple.

43. Take personality tests. Compare your answers and see how they say you're different and similar. Do you agree? Disagree? Talk about what you think. Some tests you can take for free online include Enneagram, Myers-Briggs, and Big 5.

44. Answer the 36 questions that lead to love. These questions have been put together to bring out mutual vulnerability between those who answer them. Originally created for strangers to get to know each other quickly, they're also great for you to build a closer connection with your partner. You can find the list of questions on The New York Times' website.

45. Try out different relationship apps for couples. There are a ton of these out there, all with slightly different purposes. Some well-rated apps include Paired, Evergreen, Couple Game, Gottman Card Decks, and Coral. Try out a few and see which ones you like. Continue to use your favorite(s) beyond your date night.

Sexy Time

46. Make your own massage candles. Search online for "DIY massage candle" for instructions on how to make these. You can also buy them if you don't feel like making your own. Once you light the candle, wait for the waxy oil to melt, blow it out and use the hot oil to massage each other. Be sure to check the temperature of the oil with a finger before pouring onto your partner!

47. Take a bath together. Go all out! Use bubble bath, bath bombs and candles. Dim the lights and play romantic music. You can even make your own sugar scrub using ½ cup coconut oil, ¼ cup sugar and 2 tablespoons lemon zest.

48. Dress up in fancy (or sexy) clothes and have a photo shoot. Take turns taking photos of each other using your phone or a digital camera. Then, set the camera on a tripod (or up against something steady), use the timer and take photos of yourselves together.

49. Play "Never have I ever," strip edition. Play as you normally would (search online if you need a reminder of the instructions), and each time you're guilty of having done one of the acts mentioned, remove one piece of clothing. The game ends when one of you has no clothes left to remove..

50. Learn different massage techniques and practice on each other. Search online for videos of various massage techniques that you can try on each other, including gliding and kneading.

51. Read a sexy scene from a romance novel together. You can find these online at many different websites including thegoodbits.com. After you're finishing reading, act it out!

52. Play the Game of Love bed sheet board game. This one may be easiest explained by searching online for "Game of love bed sheet game", but the gist is that you use a marker to draw game board spaces onto a bed sheet. In each space write a task you can do in bed, such as "shoulder rub" or "minus one piece of clothing". Keep playing until you get to the very last space - "SCORE!".

53. Play strip Twister. Every time one of you falls over, you must take off one piece of clothing. To make this more challenging, play with the mat on the bed.

Creative & Crafty

54. Order a custom puzzle using a photo of the two of you. Put the puzzle together during your date. You could also make a digital collage of the two of you instead of using just one photo. You can find several places that offer custom puzzle making online.

55. Make a collaborative painting together. Get a large canvas and some acrylic paints. Paint whatever strikes your fancy. Here are a few ideas: abstract, your home, your family, your pets, or your last name(s).

56. Make crafts out of Shrinky Dinks. Shrinky Dinks are thin plastic sheets that you can cut out and color and turn into plastic trinkets. Once finished decorating, pop them in the oven for a few minutes and watch them become smaller, thicker and sturdier. Try making keychains, ornaments, bookmarks or anything else you can think of.

57. Make matching t-shirts. Buy cheap blank t-shirts from a craft store, buy some fabric paint or fabric markers and design the shirts however you like. For inspiration, look up "couple shirts" images on Google.

58. Make origami for each other. Buy an origami book or follow instructions online to make folded paper animals, boxes, roses, and anything else you can imagine for each other.

59. Paint each other's portraits. Grab two medium-sized canvases and some acrylic paint from a craft store, put some newspaper or a tarp down on your kitchen table. Set up a station on each side of the table and spend your date doing your best to paint an accurate depiction of the person across from you.

60. Paint and sip at home. Wine and paint bars are widely popular and can be found in many cities across the US. You can have a similar experience at home! Search online for "paint at home kits with video." Many of these kits come with instructional videos. They come packed with everything you need - canvases, paints, brushes, and a mixing palette. Watch the video and go at your own pace. Compare your paintings and hang them on your wall.

61. Make a digital poster. Using a free graphic design website like Canva, choose a premade template and customize it to be your own. It can be a place you like, a band you like, wedding photos of the two of you, really anything. Search for "band poster" or "event poster" in Canva to see examples. Like what you made? You can order a physical print of your poster right from within Canva.

62. Sculpt objects out of clay. Buy some clay (any kind will do) from a local craft store. Or, use Play-Doh if you have some at home. Then, one of you sits at a table blindfolded. The other sits behind, guiding your partner's hands as you try to sculpt objects together, *Ghost*-style. Attempt to mold a coffee mug, a dog, or a person. Have fun!

63. Create moss wall art or a terrarium. You can find moss wall art kits on Etsy, ranging from simple to more complex. Spend your evening together building the perfect piece of living (or used-to-be living) art. Pro tip - use preserved moss instead of dried moss —it'll last longer! While not technically alive, preserved moss still has a bright green color and brings a bit of nature into your space.

64. Try out body painting. Put down a tarp, put some paints on a palette or paper plate, and take turns finger painting on each other. Clothing optional!

65. Have a tie-dye date. Buy a tie dye kit online or from a local craft store. Dye shirts, socks, underwear, tote bags - whatever you'd like. Start with white fabric and follow the instructions that come with the kit to learn how to fold and twist the fabric to get your desired look. Keep the items for yourself, or swap with your partner.

66. Draw silhouettes of each other. Tape a piece of white paper to a wall. Place a flashlight on a table facing the piece of paper. One of you sits in between the paper and the flashlight. You'll see a shadow of your silhouette on the paper. The other partner traces around the shadow. Cut the silhouette out of the white paper and place onto a piece of black construction paper. Trace the silhouette on the black construction paper and cut out. Glue the black silhouette onto white poster board. Now switch. Frame your silhouettes and put them up somewhere special - like above your bed.

67. Capture slow motion with your phones. Lots of phones have the ability to record video at high frame rates, letting you capture beautiful slow motion. Drop an egg on your kitchen counter, blow out a lit candle, use a dropper to drip oil into water, light a match, pour milk into coffee. The possibilities are endless and you don't need to go out to buy anything special. Spend your date marveling at the details of everyday events in super slow motion. Once finished, edit your clips together into a compilation video.

68. Write a story. Take turns writing a couple sentences each and pass back and forth. Read the story aloud once you feel like you've written enough and be the audience for the tale you've concocted. For a twist, try each starting a story and swapping and adding to your tales in turn.

69. Create a short film with your phones. Brainstorm a plot, characters and setting. Do you want to make a scary film? Something romantic? Or funny? After you've decided on the details, write out a one-page script (or don't and decide to ad lib the whole thing). Film the video and edit it with video editing software on your computer or phone. While you might not win any awards for your short film, it's a chance to collaborate with your partner, be creative and make something together. Look forward to watching it twenty years from now and having a good laugh.

Music & Song

70. Make music with an electronic device called Touch Me from Playtronica (buy from playtronica.com). The device allows you to make music with your partner (or anyone) by touching. Spend your date experimenting. What sounds can you make together?

73. Make a joint Spotify or YouTube playlist. Choose songs that are meaningful to the two of you.

71. Make a song. Use real instruments if you have them or make instruments from items around the house (tissue box and rubber band guitar, anyone?). Spend your date making up the music and lyrics together and record a version of your improvised or written song with the voice recorder or voice memos app on your phone. If you want to step it up a notch, bring the recording into an audio editing program like Garageband and add beats or looping vocals.

72. Watch your favorite bands' past concerts. YouTube has a plethora of these. Search for "Band Name" + "Full Concert" and see what you can find.

74. Have a karaoke date.. YouTube is a great resource for karaoke song videos. They'll give you the lyrics and background music and you just follow along. For a compilation of karaoke song videos, search for "Scan and Sing Karaoke Book" on Amazon. It lists out a ton of popular karaoke songs and pairs each with a QR code. Use your phone to scan the code. When the video pops up on your phone, cast it to your TV. Simple as that.

Move Your Bodies

75. Do partner yoga. There are lots of blog articles online and videos on YouTube with ideas of different yoga poses specifically for two people. Just search for "partner yoga" or "couples yoga." White not necessarily just for couples, doing yoga together is a great way to be close to each other physically while also getting some exercise.

76. Take an online dance class. There are tons of virtual dance classes offered in every different style of dance you can think of. The Passion4dancing YouTube channel is a great place to start. Try your hand (or foot?) at salsa, swing, bachata - you name it!

77. Have a silent dance party. Agree on a a dance or pop playlist from Spotify or YouTube. You and your partner each put on headphones, hit play at the same time on your devices and dance your cares away.

78. Do a partner workout. Search YouTube for "partner workout" or "couples workout" and you'll find good options for getting exercise while still being close to your partner. Most of the exercises require you and your partner working together to accomplish the workout. It's a fun way to get the blood pumping, feel healthy and collaborate with your partner.

79. Sumo wrestle. Grab some old, oversized t-shirts and pillows. Have each of you put on a shirt, stuff them with pillows and pretend you are sumo wrestlers. (Gently) run into each other and see who can pin the other to the ground.

Explore the World

80. Explore the world from the comfort of your home. Use Google street view or Google Earth to take "walks" in different places around the world. Is there a special place you'd like to visit but maybe it's not feasible to go right now? Check it out virtually. Virtual reality apps like Wander can also fully immerse you in your new location.

81. Book an Airbnb online experience. Airbnb isn't just for booking travel accommodations. They also have some really great local experiences in cities across the world. In addition to offering in-person experiences, they also have many virtual offerings as well. These can range from virtual tours of cities around the world with local guides to virtual cooking classes and trip planning with a local. Start out by going to airbnb.com and click on "Online Experiences" at the top of the page and discover something new to try.

82. Go on a virtual museum tour. Many museums around the world offer virtual tours. so explore these rich stores of knowledge without having to get on a plane - or even leave your house! Some favorites include the British Museum of London, The Guggenheim of New York, and the Uffizi Gallery in Florence. Pop open your laptop and "walk" around the museum. Discuss any works of art you or your partner find particularly fascinating.

83. Plan a fake vacation together. Choose a location that both of you have always wanted to go to. Research places to stay and things to do. No need to hold back - choose the most elaborate hotels, the all-inclusive options, the private island tour - with no worry of what it would actually cost! Spend your date looking through pictures and watch videos of activities you'd like to do and pretend you're there.

84. Play the Geoguessr game and find out who knows their geography better. Using Google Street View, the online game Geoguessr places you in a random location somewhere in the world. Take turns guessing where you are on the map. The game shows how far away you actually are. Whoever's guess comes closest each round wins!

Just For Fun

85. Break a record together. Look at the Guiness Book of World Records website (guinessworldrecords.com), or find the latest edition of the book at the library. Find a record you think you could break together and go for it! Make sure you read the rules about what to do and how to apply if you're actually serious about this one.

86. Spend the evening unplugged. Put your phones away and turn off the lights. Pretend you have no electricity and get creative with how you'll spend the evening. Reading together with flashlights? A candlelit bath? Straight to the bedroom? It's up to you!

87. Watch your favorite childhood movies or TV shows together. Are there any similarities between yours and your partner's picks? See if your childhood favorites stand the test of time or if they were better when you were a kid.

88. Have a Zoom double date with another couple. Play a game together like trivia, share a glass of wine virtually, or just chat and catch up.

89. Perform your own science experiments. There are tons of YouTube videos and blog posts with different experiments for you to try at home. Most of these will say they're for kids, but they can be just as fun as an adult! Try instant freezing a water bottle, crystallize your own rock candy or grow a carbon sugar snake. Check out the YouTube channel 5-Minute Magic for plenty of ideas.

90. Spend the evening stargazing. Grab some blankets or outdoor chairs and head to your backyard. Look up at the sky and stargaze. Are you able to spot any constellations? For extra fun, look up a meteor shower calendar and see if you can spot a shooting star.

91. Have a comedy night at home. Watch comedy specials from your favorite comedians on Netflix or YouTube. Afterward, each try your hand at writing jokes. Take turns performing your sets and see who laughs the hardest.

92. Watch motivational speeches on YouTube. With your partner, browse through motivational speeches. Agree on two or three to watch together. Discuss after watching: do you agree with the speakers? Do you feel motivated? End the date by writing a motivational speech together based on everything you've learned.

93. Read a new (or favorite) book out loud together. Take turns reading a few paragraphs each and switching off. Discuss what you read. Is it harder to pay attention to the story while reading or listening?

94. Volunteer from home. Search justserve.org for several remote volunteering opportunities. Spend the date with your partner writing letters to people in prison or decorating pillowcases for kids in the hospital.

95. Have a seasonal date. Celebrate each other and your favorite seasons! Carve pumpkins. Gather the fixin's for a hot chocolate bar. Tackle spring cleaning around your home. Have an indoor BBQ with watermelon, brats and cold beer.

96. Take turns telling each other scary stories. Either read from a book of scary stories or make up your own. Turn off the lights and hold a flashlight under your chin (of course) for added effect.

97. Enjoy a zen evening of meditation. Set the mood by dimming the lights, lighting candles and playing calming music. Sit on pillows on the floor or upright in chairs. Play a guided meditation video from YouTube (or the *Headspace* guided meditation on Netflix), or simply set a timer and sit until the meditation ends. You'll feel your stress from the day float away.

98. Turn your bedroom into a hotel room. Put on your pajamas or your robes, order "room service" (take out), eat on the bed, and turn on the TV and flip through the channels.

99. Watch a drive-in movie in your driveway. Head outside with a fully-charged laptop. Sit in your car with the windows down and place your laptop on the hood. Turn the volume up on your laptop speakers, cuddle up close and enjoy the show.

100. Invite another couple over for a game night. Who says date night has to just be the two of you? Choose a few multiplayer board games (or video games) and spend some time bonding with another couple as you puzzle out rules together. Ticket to Ride, Splendor, and Forbidden Island are a few options that are good for small groups.

101. Watch a documentary. It can be a topic you're familiar with and want to learn more about, or covering material you know nothing about. Take time after watching to discuss with your partner. Was it interesting? Did you learn anything new? What surprised you? What, if any changes would you consider making after watching the documentary?

Conclusion

I hope you enjoyed these 101 at-home date night ideas.

Hopefully you found some new ideas to try. See? You don't have to leave home or spend much money to have a great date.

If you found it helpful, I'd appreciate it very much if you left a favorable review for this book on Amazon.

Resources

Challenge, S. O. T. A. (2021). The Adventure Challenge Couples Edition - 50 Scratch-Off Adventures & Date Night Games for Couples, Couples Scratch Off Book, Couples Adventure Book for Anniversary or Wedding Gift. The Adventure Challenge.

Conversation Starters World. (n.d.). 200 Date Ideas. Retrieved July 12, 2022, from https://conversationstartersworld.com/date-ideas/

McAfee, T. (2022, February 2). 45 At-Home Date Night Ideas to Reignite Your Romance. The Pioneer Woman. Retrieved July 12, 2022, from https://www.thepioneerwoman.com/home-lifestyle/a77897/at-home-date-night-ideas/

Oh Delicioso. (2018, June 22). Gourmet S'mores - Four Ways. Retrieved July 12, 2022, from https://ohsodelicioso.com/gourmet-smores-four-ways/

Riley, J. (2021, July 6). 50 CREATIVE AND FUN AT HOME DATE NIGHT IDEAS PERFECT FOR PARENTS. Confidence Meets Parenting. Retrieved July 12, 2022, from https://confidencemeetsparenting.com/date-night-ideas/

So Festive. (n.d.). 55 AT-HOME DATE IDEAS THAT ARE ACTUALLY FUN. Retrieved July 12, 2022, from https://sofestive.com/2021/01/07/at-hom e-date-ideas/

The Yellow Birdhouse. (2021, June 11). 29 Fun At Home Date Night Ideas for Parents. Retrieved July 12, 2022, from https://www.theyellowbirdho use.com/29-fun-at-home-date-night-ideas-for-parents/

Made in United States
Troutdale, OR
09/25/2024